HISTORY'S FAMOUS FEUDS

Adolf Hitler and Winston Churchill

Rivals of World War II

Lindsey Lowe

Enslow PUBLISHING

Published in 2024 by Enslow Publishing, LLC
2544 Clinton Street
Buffalo, NY 14224

Portions of this work were originally authored by Ellis Roxburgh and published as *Adolf Hitler vs. Winston Churchill: Foes of World War II*. All new material this edition authored by Lindsey Lowe.

Children's Publisher: Anne O'Daly
Design Manager: Keith Davis
Picture Manager: Sophie Mortimer

Manufactured in the United States of America

CPSIA compliance information: Batch #CSENS24: For further information contact Enslow Publishing LLC, New York, New York at 1-800-398-2504.

Please visit our website, www.enslowpublishing.com. For a free color catalog of all our high-quality books, call toll free 1-800-398-2504 or fax 1-877-980-4454.

Cataloging-in-Publication Data

Names: Lowe, Lindsey.
Title: Adolf Hitler and Winston Churchill: rivals of World War II / Lindsey Lowe.
Description: New York : Enslow Publishing, 2024. | Series: History's famous feuds | Includes index.
Identifiers: ISBN 9781978536449 (pbk.) | ISBN 9781978536456 (library bound) | ISBN 9781978536463 (ebook)
Subjects: LCSH: Hitler, Adolf, 1889-1945--Juvenile literature. | Churchill, Winston, 1874-1965--Juvenile literature. | World War, 1939-1945--Juvenile literature.
Classification: LCC D743.7 O34 2024 | DDC 940.53--dc23

Front Cover: Library and Archives Canada: right, Shutterstock: Elzbieta Sekowska, left.

All images Robert Hunt Library except:
Library and Archives Canada 5, 43, odd numbers tr, 11-27, 31, 33, 37-4;
Shutterstock: Elzbieta Sekowska 4, 42, even numbers tl, 10-26, 30, 32, 36-40; Topfoto: Roger-Viollet 41.

t=top, b=bottom, l=left, r=right

Artistic Effects
Shutterstock

Contents

Facing Off

Adolf Hitler V Winston Churchill

Adolf Hitler (1889–1945) had fought in World War I (1914–1918). He became leader of the Nazi Party in the 1920s and rose to become the chancellor, or leader, of Germany in early 1933.

- Hitler believed the Allies had been victorious in World War I because German politicians had given in when they should have stood firm.
- He wanted to bring all Germans together in a single country and to create a new German empire.
- He invaded Poland in 1939. France and Great Britain declared war on Germany in order to protect Poland.

The man who became the symbol of Britain during World War II (1939–1945) was Prime Minister Winston Churchill (1874–1965). Many British people were suspicious of Churchill because of mistakes he had made in the past.

» Churchill had been a soldier and a war reporter before he was elected as a Conservative Member of Parliament in 1900.

» During World War I, Churchill was in charge of the Royal Navy. He was fired after he helped plan a disastrous invasion of Turkey.

» At the start of World War II, he again took charge of the navy.

» He became Prime Minister in 1940. His refusal to give in to Germany inspired the British people.

Background

In 1918, Germany and the western Allies—the United States, Britain, and France—agreed an end to World War I. Britain and France were determined to make Germany pay for the war.

After the war ended on November 11, 1918, the Allies, and France and Britain in particular, demanded that Germany pay huge fines, called reparations. Observers such as U.S. President Woodrow Wilson did not think this was wise. Germany was one of Europe's largest countries. If its economy was left ruined and weak, it would not be able to trade, which would damage the economies of its neighbors.

A Harsh Treaty

Despite such warnings, the Treaty of Versailles (1919) set out Germany's punishment for starting the war. Germany was ordered to pay the equivalent of 33 billion dollars in fines and lost 13 percent of its pre-war territory. Its army was dramatically reduced in size, and it was forbidden to manufacture armaments such as planes or warships. Many Germans felt they had been humiliated on the world stage. The scene was set for discontent and conflict.

TRENCHES: The German Army was defeated on the Western Front.

1920s Germany

Postwar Germany was a terrible place. There were shortages of food and no jobs. The economy was in ruins. In the chaos, small communist and right-wing groups sprang up. In Russia, there had been a communist revolution in 1917. Many Germans feared that a revolution might also break out in Germany.

BURNING: German money became so worthless it was burned as fuel.

Hitler in Charge

In September 1919, the army sent a World War I veteran named Adolf Hitler to observe a small right-wing group named the German Workers' Party. Hitler soon began to take part in its meetings. He was a gifted speaker who drew big crowds. The party listened to Hitler's ideas about how to make it more popular. These included changing its name to the National Socialist German Workers' Party, or Nazis for short. Hitler chose red as the party's color in order to annoy the communists, who always used red. He also introduced the swastika as the party's symbol.

> "People need a good scare. They want to be afraid of something, they want someone to make them afraid."
>
> **Adolf Hitler, 1923**

Mussolini in Italy

Germany was not the only country in chaos after World War I. In Italy, a communist revolution also seemed possible. In 1922, Benito Mussolini (1883–1945) became Italy's prime minister. In 1925, he turned Italy into a dictatorship run according to his fascist ideas. Mussolini believed that individual freedom and democracy should be sacrificed for the good of the country. Hitler greatly admired what Mussolini was doing in Italy.

Important Year

The year 1923 was critical for Hitler's rise to power. After Germany failed to pay its reparation payments on time, France occupied its most important industrial region, the Ruhr, and took control of its mines and factories. As a result, the German economy collapsed.

FASCIST: Mussolini came to power in Italy after marching on Rome with his supporters in 1922.

> "The best way to take control over a people and control them utterly is to take a little of their freedom at a time."
>
> **Adolf Hitler, 1923**

PARADE: The Nazis used increasingly large military parades to attract supporters.

Prices rose so fast that the mark, Germany's currency, became worthless. People lost their life savings overnight. The bank printed banknotes for millions of marks that were not enough to buy even a loaf of bread. Membership of the Nazi Party grew from 20,000 members at the start of 1923 to 55,000 by its end.

Hitler's Failed Revolution

Hitler decided the time was right to stage a revolution. With his armed followers, he tried to overthrow the state government in Bavaria. The revolution failed. Hitler was arrested and sent to jail. In court, he used his chance to repeat his political ideas. He blamed an international conspiracy for Germany's problems. He said the main conspirators were the Jews. He claimed that the German Army had not been defeated in World War I, but rather betrayed by liberal politicians. He said that Germany had to fight against the terms of the Versailles Treaty. He used his time in prison to repeat these ideas in a book entitled *Mein Kampf* (My Struggle). It contained most of the ideas he later put into practice.

Adolf Hitler

» DRIVEN BY BITTERNESS

Adolf Hitler was born in Austria in 1889. His failure to get into art school made him bitter. He moved to Germany in 1913.

SUPPORTERS: One of Hitler's gifts was making speeches in front of huge crowds.

Hitler was born in a small town in Austria. His father was a bully who was devoted to the Hapsburg monarchy that ruled the Austro-Hungarian Empire. In 1907, Adolf Hitler moved to the capital, Vienna, to try to become an artist. When he failed to get into art school, he ended up living in a hostel for homeless men. This experience made him resentful of what he saw as the indulgent lifestyle of people in Vienna.

Move to Germany

In 1913, Hitler arrived in Munich, the capital of the southern German state of Bavaria. When World War I broke out in 1914, he volunteered to join the German Army. He was promoted to corporal and was awarded the Iron Cross, Germany's highest military award, for serving on the Western Front.

Joining the Party

When the war ended in 1918, Hitler was in hospital suffering from temporary blindness following a British gas attack. When he recovered he worked for the German Army. His job was to spy on political parties, including the German Workers' Party (DAP). Hitler was attracted to the DAP's anti-communist, anti-Semitic, right-wing ideas, and he quit the army to join it. By 1921, he had become the party leader.

PARTY: When Hitler took over the German Workers' Party, he was surrounded by army veterans.

“Every generation should take part in a war at least once.”

Adolf Hitler, 1918

Winston Churchill

» DESTINED FOR A CAREER IN POLITICS

Churchill was from a wealthy family. His ancestors included aristocrats, successful generals, and politicians.

Churchill became prime minister on May 10, 1940, eight months after World War II began. Although he was 65, he was thought to be the only man for the job. For much of the 1930s, he had tried to warn Europeans about the threat Hitler posed to democracy. He had realized that war was unavoidable soon after Hitler came to power.

Privileged Upbringing

Churchill's ancestors had been the Dukes of Marlborough, and he was brought up in the family's stately home, Blenheim Palace. His mother, Jennie, was an American heiress. Winston Churchill become a Member of Parliament for the

ARMY: Churchill took a close interest in military and naval affairs.

Conservative Party at the age of 25. By 1910, he had switched political party and was Home Secretary. Churchill served in World War I as First Lord of the Admiralty, but was fired after his planned invasion of Turkey was a failure. He later worked as a journalist before going back into politics. By now, he had a reputation for not being entirely trustworthy and for compromising his principles for the sake of personal advantage.

The Nazi Threat

When Churchill visited Germany in 1932, Hitler refused to meet him. Churchill already knew that Hitler was dangerous, and repeatedly warned of the threat of Nazism. When Churchill became Britain's prime minister in May 1940, he seemed the only man who could stop Hitler.

MP: Churchill's political career was always full of controversy.

> "Hitler constitutes the greatest danger for the British Empire."
>
> **Winston Churchill, 1936**

Hitler's Inner Circle

» AN ABSOLUTE RULER

Hitler prized loyalty above any other quality in his closest advisors. He operated a policy of "divide and rule" to keep absolute power.

DINNER: Hitler (right) talks to Joseph Goebbels, the Nazis' minister for propaganda, late in World War II.

Hitler had a reputation for being able to charm the people he met. He inspired great loyalty in those who worked for him. He was a kind employer who remembered their names and their birthdays. But he also used threats to keep his advisors desperate to please him.

Loyal Supporters

Hitler's most senior advisors were those men who had worked with him longest. They included Hermann Göring (1893–1946), head of the Luftwaffe, or German Air Force. Göring had joined Hitler's German Workers' Party in 1922.

HIMMLER: Heinrich Himmler (standing) was Hitler's head of security.

> “Hitler's decisions... were only made to demonstrate to the head of the Army that Hitler was in command and nobody else.”
>
> **Major Gerhard Engel**

Heinrich Himmler (1900–1945) had taken part in Hitler's failed Bavarian revolution in 1923. Himmler became the second most powerful man in the Nazi Party and ran the feared SS, Hitler's paramilitary bodyguard. Joseph Goebbels (1897–1945), the minister for propaganda, was another early supporter of Nazi beliefs. Goebbels was highly effective at convincing German citizens that Hitler's policies would be good for Germany.

Flawed Judgment

Hitler overruled even his best generals. This led to strategic errors during the war, such as his decision to invade the Soviet Union in June 1941. Hitler's "divide and rule" policy meant his generals did not share information. They often gave Hitler the advice he wanted to hear, rather than the best advice for a situation.

Churchill's Friends

» INTERNATIONAL ALLIES

Churchill chose his advisors carefully. He got on well with most Allied leaders, especially Franklin D. Roosevelt.

GENERALS: Churchill had great trust in his leading generals.

Churchill was often gruff and outspoken, but he was also ready to admit when he was in the wrong. He took advice from his generals, such as Bernard Montgomery and the U.S. general Dwight D. Eisenhower, who was Supreme Commander of the Allied forces.

Realistic Aims

Churchill was a realist. He was prepared to do whatever was necessary to get results. Clement Attlee, for example, was leader of the Labour Party, making him Churchill's political opponent in Britain. But Churchill knew everyone had to work together for victory, so he made Attlee his deputy.

Special Relationship

As war grew closer, Churchill developed a particularly close relationship with U.S. President Franklin D. Roosevelt. When the United States declared war on Germany following the attack on Pearl Harbor on December 7, 1941, Churchill was relieved. He believed it meant that Britain could now win the war.

Reluctant Ally

Churchill was reluctant to work with Joseph Stalin of the Soviet Union. Stalin was a cruel dictator. But Churchill decided it was better to work with Stalin in order to present a united front against Germany rather than risk weakening the Allied cause.

THREE: The "Big Three" meet in 1945 (from left): Winston Churchill, Franklin D. Roosevelt, and Joseph Stalin.

"I felt I was in contact with a very great man who was also a warmhearted friend."

Winston Churchill on Franklin D. Roosevelt

Tension in Europe

» GERMANY TEARS UP THE TREATY OF VERSAILLES

In 1933, Hitler became chancellor of Germany. He did not take the position by force but was elected by the people.

SUCCESS: Hitler used his popularity to force President Hindenburg to make him chancellor.

After the failure of his attempt to overthrow the Bavarian government in 1923, Hitler decided to take power by democratic means. He won support for the Nazis with his message that Germany's problems were the fault of the Jews and communists, or "Bolsheviks" as he called them.

Preparation for War

Hitler's electoral success grew until 1933, when he had enough support to force President Hindenburg to appoint him chancellor. Hitler used elections to cement his power and then moved to crush opposition to the Nazi Party, becoming a dictator. He even murdered 150 of his former Nazi colleagues during what was later known as the "Night of the Long Knives" on June 30, 1934.

Germany Takes the Sudetenland

Soon, despite the Treaty of Versailles, Hitler was investing heavily in industry and rearmament. He also reintroduced conscription in 1935. He claimed that Germany needed more space (**Lebensraum**) and seized the Sudetenland, a German-speaking part of Czechoslovakia. He reassured the British and French that he had no other plans, so they did not stop him. This was called appeasement. However, Hitler soon invaded the rest of Czechoslovakia and, as Churchill had long been warning, war now appeared almost certain.

"An appeaser is one who feeds a crocodile, hoping it will eat him last."

Winston Churchill, 1938

ARMS: Hitler broke the terms of the Versailles Treaty in order to rearm the Germany Army.

Invasion of Poland

FLASHPOINT » HITLER STRIKES EAST

Hitler wanted to invade Poland. To do so, he made an alliance with the Soviet Union and attacked in September 1939.

BORDER: German soldiers pull down a barrier at the border with Poland.

At the 1938 Munich Conference, Hitler had convinced the French and British to allow him to annex part of Czechoslovakia. When he later seized the rest of the country, France and Britain still did nothing. Both countries had promised to defend Poland if Hitler attacked it, but Hitler was confident neither country would be prepared to risk war with Germany. He thought they were too weak. In March 1939, he ordered his generals to prepare to invade Poland.

PANZER: A German Panzer, or tank, rolls through the Polish countryside in 1939.

The Nazi-Soviet Pact

On August 23, 1939, Germany and the Soviet Union signed a pact. A secret part of the pact agreed that they would invade Poland and divide the country between them. On August 31, German soldiers dressed in Polish uniforms attacked Germany from Poland. This gave Hitler his excuse to invade Poland.

Invasion and War

On September 1, 1939, 1.5 million German soldiers crossed the border into Poland. Britain and France declared war on Germany on September 3. On September 17, the Russians attacked from the east. By the end of the month, Poland no longer existed and Britain and Germany were at war.

> "When starting and waging a war it is not right that matters, but victory."
>
> **Adolf Hitler, August 1939**

Miracle at Dunkirk

FLASHPOINT » RESCUING THE ARMY

After the invasion of Poland, German troops overran northwest Europe. The British Army was cut off in northern France.

BEACHES: Stranded British and French troops wait to be evacuated from the beach at Dunkirk.

On May 10, 1940, Winston Churchill became prime minister of Britain. The same day, Hitler invaded France, Belgium, the Netherlands, and Luxembourg. Within a week Churchill faced a grave emergency.

Escape by Sea

The British Expeditionary Force sent to help France was being pushed back toward the English Channel. The British and French armies in Europe were retreating with the Germans close behind until on May 24 Hitler suddenly ordered his army to stop. Two days later, Hitler changed his mind and ordered the advance to continue. But the break had given the British soldiers a vital chance to escape.

Flotilla of Little Ships

Churchill appealed for boat owners to cross the English Channel and help rescue the British and French troops from the beaches and harbors of Dunkirk. Some 338,000 men were saved, although they had to abandon their equipment. France surrendered on June 18, 1940. Now Britain stood alone against Germany—but Churchill had saved the British Army.

> "The battle beginning today will decide the fate of the German nation for the next thousand years."
>
> **Adolf Hitler, 1940**

FLOTILLA: Hundreds of tiny boats set off from Britain to rescue soldiers from French beaches.

War in the Air

FLASHPOINT » THE BATTLE OF BRITAIN

When France surrendered in summer 1940, Hitler wanted to invade Britain. But first he had to destroy the Royal Air Force (RAF).

SCRAMBLE: RAF pilots rush for their aircraft to face a German attack.

Hermann Göring assured Hitler that his Luftwaffe pilots could defeat the British airmen. Churchill warned, "I expect that the battle of Britain is just beginning. Upon this battle depends the survival of Christian civilization." In almost constant battles from late July until October 1940, the RAF and Luftwaffe pilots fought in the skies above England. German bombers accompanied by fighter escorts attacked from France and across the North Sea from bases in Norway.

Speed, Agility, and Radar

British airmen and their allies from France, Poland, and the Commonwealth "scrambled" to their fighters on airfields all over southern Britain. Although the Germans had more planes, the British Hurricanes and Spitfires more than matched them in speed and agility. The British also had the benefit of a new invention, radar, which warned of the arrival of German planes.

German Failure

The Germans targeted industrial sites, supply lines, and RAF bases, but the strategy failed. By the end of September 1940, the Germans had failed to gain air superiority and plans for an invasion by sea were cancelled.

> "Never in the field of human conflict was so much owed by so many to so few."
>
> **Winston Churchill, 1940**

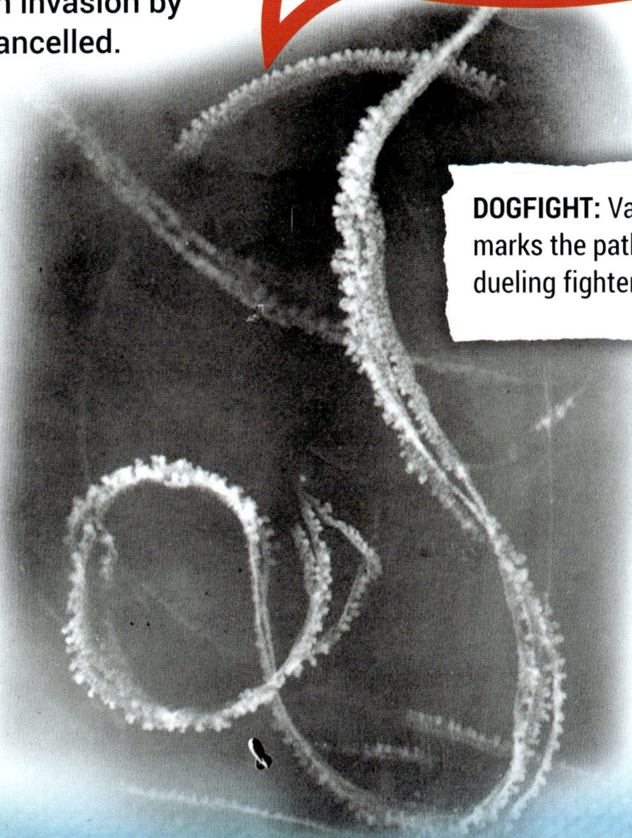

DOGFIGHT: Vapor marks the paths of dueling fighter planes.

Bombing Britain

FLASHPOINT » THE BLITZ ON BRITAIN

After he had failed to destroy the RAF, Hitler tried to destroy Britain's cities in a bombing campaign the British called the "Blitz."

CRATER: Londoners examine bomb damage outside the Bank of England.

"These cruel, wanton, indiscriminate bombings of London are a part of Hitler's invasion plans."

Winston Churchill, September 1940

By the late summer of 1940, Hitler realized that he did not yet have the air superiority to invade Britain. Instead, he ordered the Luftwaffe to bomb British cities. The following period of intense bombing is known as the Blitz, German for "lightning."

Air Attacks

Both sides had already bombed enemy territory before, but from September 7, 1940, German

bombers switched to attacking at night in order to avoid airplane losses during daylight raids. The German bombers returned almost every night for 267 days, until May 21, 1941. They struck London in 71 raids, including a period of 57 nights in a row. A million homes were destroyed in London alone. The city also suffered about half of the total 40,000 civilian deaths during the Blitz. German bombers also targeted strategic cities, such as the ports of Liverpool and Hull. The aim of the bombing was to destroy Britain's war economy and damage British morale.

Nightly Raids

Life in London soon took on a grim routine. When the air-raid sirens sounded or at bedtime, Londoners quickly made for shelter. Some had corrugated-iron "Anderson" shelters dug into the backyard. Others headed for the subway stations.

SPOTTERS: Air raid wardens in London look out for fires started by German bombs.

> “Little does Hitler know the spirit of the British nation, or the tough fiber of the Londoners.”
>
> **Winston Churchill, September 1940**

BOMBER: A German bomber flies high above the Thames River in London’s docklands.

By the end of September 1940, almost 200,000 Londoners slept on the platforms of the subway every night. Those who were able to left the city and moved to the countryside.

“V for Victory”

Throughout the Blitz, Churchill remained in London. He toured the bomb sites, inspecting the damage and giving his famous two-finger “V for Victory” sign. This made him very popular. Churchill's behavior was in stark contrast to Hitler's. Later in the war, Hitler refused to visit Germany's bombed-out cities because he thought it made him look weak.

The Biggest Raid

The most damaging of the London raids came on December 29, 1940. Around 130 German planes caused a huge fire known as the Second Great Fire of London (the first was in 1666). St. Paul's Cathedral survived and became a symbol of Britain's refusal to surrender.

Blitz Abandoned

By May 1941, Hitler realized the Blitz had failed. British morale remained high. By now he was planning to invade the Soviet Union, for which he needed ammunition, airplanes, and pilots. In May 1941, the long air campaign against Britain was finally abandoned.

SYMBOL: The dome of St. Paul's Cathedral rises above the smoke and flames after a bombing raid.

El Alamein

FLASHPOINT » TURNING POINT IN AFRICA

There were many battles in North Africa, where Britain fought against Germany and its Italian ally.

SURRENDER: A German tanker surrenders to a British infantryman.

The German Afrika Korps was commanded by the oustanding general Irwin Rommel. Nicknamed the "Desert Fox," he pushed the British 8th Army and its allies back through the Libyan desert in late 1941 and early 1942. Churchill ordered that the vital port of Tobruk be held at all costs, but it fell to the Germans in June 1942. Hitler promoted Rommel, who became the youngest field marshal in the German Army.

Egypt Under Threat

By June 1942, the Germans threatened El Alamein in western Egypt. A victory there would give them access to the oilfields of the Middle East. It would also wreck the Allies' plan of using North Africa to launch an invasion of southern Europe.

Montgomery Turns the Tide

In a first battle in June, the British halted Rommel's advance. Churchill gave the 8th Army a new commander, General Bernard Montgomery, and more equipment and men. In the Battle of El Alamein, in October and November, Montgomery won a huge victory. Churchill was jubilant. He knew that the victory was a vital turning point in the war.

> "Before Alamein we never had a victory. After Alamein we never had a defeat."
>
> **Winston Churchill, 1951**

PRISONERS: A single British armored car keeps guard over hundreds of captured Germans.

D-Day

FLASHPOINT » INVADING EUROPE

As the war swung in favor of the Allies, Britain and the United States prepared to invade France and march to Germany.

In August 1942, the Soviet dictator, Joseph Stalin, asked Winston Churchill and U.S. president Franklin D. Roosevelt to open a new front in the west to take pressure off the Eastern Front. The Allies began preparations for an eventual invasion. The Germans built a series of defenses along the 700-mile (1,130 km) coast of France. Hitler was convinced the invasion would come near Calais in northern France. Although his generals disagreed, he ordered most of the defensive troops to be concentrated there.

FLEET: Landing craft carry the invasion force across the English Channel.

AIRBORNE: Gliders land Allied troops in Normandy early on D-Day.

June 6, 1944

However, since 1943, U.S. and British troops had been preparing for a landing on the beaches of Normandy, far from Calais. By late spring 1944, all the hardware and personnel were assembled, but Allies had to wait for good weather before setting the date: June 6, 1944. While it was still dark, thousands of airborne soldiers were dropped in Normandy to seize key targets. At the same time, a fleet of more than 5,000 vessels crossed the English Channel from Britain. After a massive sea and air bombardment, Allied troops started to land on the beaches as dawn broke. German resistance varied across the five beaches, but Allied casualties were heaviest on Omaha and Utah Beaches.

"The free men of the world are marching together to victory... We will accept nothing less than full victory. Good luck!"

General Dwight D. Eisenhower, June 1944

Taken by Surprise

The Germans were caught unprepared. Rommel, who was now in charge of the Channel defenses, was in Germany. Hitler, still believing the main landing would come in Calais, held back his tank reserves. By the time he released them, it was too late. As the fighting continued on the first day, Allied air supremacy meant that the German tanks came under heavy attack as they approached the landing beaches.

> *"Your task will not be an easy one. Your enemy is well trained, well equipped, and battle hardened. He will fight savagely."*
>
> **General Dwight D. Eisenhower, June 1944**

WADING: British soldiers wade chest-deep as they leave their landing craft.

BEACH: British soldiers come ashore, helping those who have been wounded during the landing.

Allied Success

By the end of June 6, the Allies had a foothold in Europe. In the coming days, hundreds of thousands more troops crossed the English Channel to reinforce the attack. As the Allies pushed into northern France, they met stiff opposition from the Germans. But within weeks more than a million Allied troops in France were outnumbering their enemy.

The fighting in Normandy would last until August, but D-Day marked the beginning of the end of the Nazi occupation of Europe. Rommel wrote to Hitler suggesting he end the war, but Hitler rejected the idea. Meanwhile Churchill visited the beachhead to celebrate with his victorious generals.

Death of Hitler

» THE DICTATOR COMMITS SUICIDE

Hitler refused to negotiate with his enemies. He took shelter beneath the parliament building in Berlin as the Allies closed in.

FAREWELL: In one of the last photographs of Hitler, he meets members of the Hitler Youth.

By early 1945, it was clear that Germany would lose the war. Soviet armies were advancing from the east, while the British and Americans had crossed the Rhine River and entered Germany in the west.

Battle for Berlin

Joseph Stalin had made a deal with the other Allies that his Red Army should be allowed to enter

Berlin first. He sent 2.5 million Soviet troops and 6,000 tanks to capture the German capital. The fighting was fierce but ended in a decisive victory for the Soviets. Hitler and his associates took shelter in his bunker, an underground complex of around 30 small rooms.

The End

On April 28, 1945, Hitler married his girlfriend, Eva Braun. Two days later she took a deadly cyanide pill and Hitler shot himself in the head. His followers waited for a lull in fighting and took the bodies aboveground. They burned them to keep them from being taken by the Soviets. On May 2, Berlin surrendered. On May 8, all the remaining German forces in Europe formally surrendered.

> "If you win, you need not have to explain... If you lose, you should not be there to explain."
>
> **Adolf Hitler, 1923**

BERLIN: Soviet troops watch the German parliament building burning.

Elder Statesman

» CHURCHILL ON THE WORLD STAGE

Churchill was extremely popular in 1945, but his political party was not. He was voted out of office, but was reelected in 1951.

FUNERAL: Churchill was given a state funeral, usually reserved for monarchs.

With Germany defeated, Churchill was seen as a hero around the world. He joined the royal family to greet Londoners celebrating Victory in Europe Day on May 8, 1945. But now that the war was over, the British people wanted a change.

Lost Election

Only two months after the end of World War II, Winston Churchill lost his job as prime minister. Clement Attlee's Labour Party won the general election. Although Churchill was reelected as Prime Minister in 1951, he was old by then and his government achieved very little.

International Expert

However, Churchill continued to be a leading voice in international affairs. He predicted the start of the Cold War when he warned that Stalin's expansion plans would lead to an "iron curtain" dividing Europe. He called for closer ties between Britain and the United States and for the creation of "a council of Europe" to help avoid future wars.

He died on January 24, 1965, at the age of 90. The British gave him a state funeral in gratitude for all that he had done for the country in its fight against Hitler.

> "You are no longer Prime Minister, but you are still Winston Churchill, which is much more, and something much better."
>
> **R. Gillon, Belgian president, 1946**

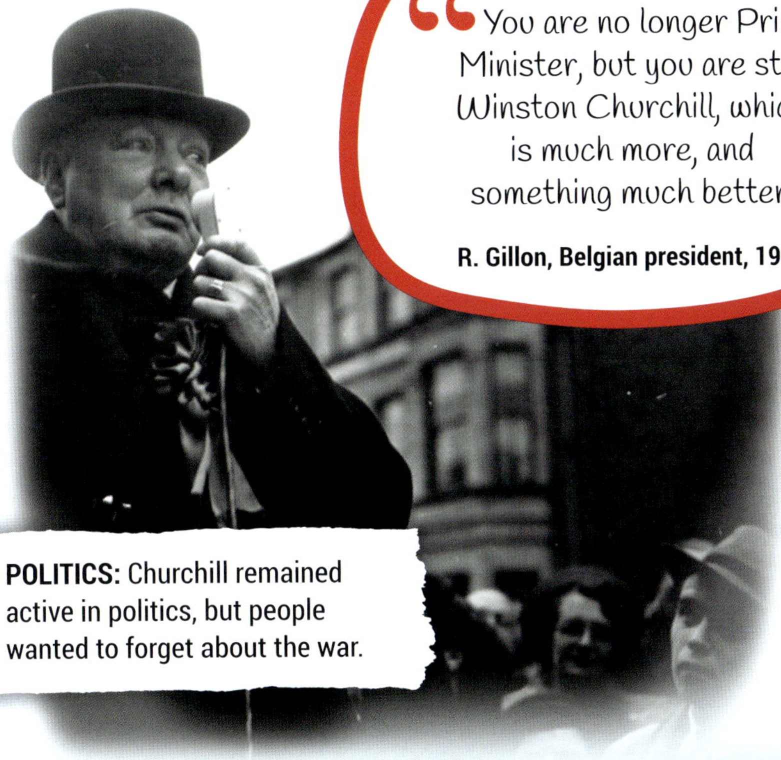

POLITICS: Churchill remained active in politics, but people wanted to forget about the war.

Aftermath

» THE WORLD DIVIDED

As the world recovered from World War II, the United States and the Soviet Union began a period of rivalry called the Cold War.

WALL: In 1961, the Russians built a massive concrete wall to divide East and West Berlin.

The Allied leaders—Roosevelt, Churchill, and Stalin—had met in February 1945 to discuss postwar Europe. By the time the war ended, however, Roosevelt was dead. Shortly afterward, Churchill lost his job. Of the "Big Three," only Stalin remained in power—and he took the lead in Europe. Soviet troops occupied much of eastern Europe. Germany was split into communist-occupied East Germany and the Allied-controlled West.

RUINED: As had happened after World War I, the German economy was left in ruins in the aftermath of World War II.

"From Stettin in the Baltic to Triestein in the Adriatic, an iron curtain has descended across the continent."

Winston Churchill, 1946

The German capital, Berlin, lay deep inside East Germany. Each of the former allies—the United States, the Soviet Union, Britain, and France—controlled its own part of the city.

The Soviet Empire

Stalin was determined that the Soviet Union would never again suffer as it had in World War II. He set about creating a "buffer zone" between Russia and the West. Over the next decade, he imposed communist governments on most of eastern Europe. Again Churchill warned of the threat a despotic leader posed to Europe—but this time the threat came from Stalin rather than Hitler.

Final Judgment

Adolf Hitler V Winston Churchill

Hitler had promised to build a reich, or empire, that would last 1,000 years. Instead it lasted only 12 years before the fall of Berlin left it in ruins. It took decades for Germany to recover from the war.

- Hitler's refusal to trust his generals led him to make a series of strategic blunders that hastened Germany's defeat.
- His policies led to the Holocaust, the murder of millions of Jews and prisoners of war.
- He is remembered as one of the great villains of history: a bigot, dictator, and war criminal who cost the lives of millions of people.

With Hitler's death and the Allied victory in the war, Churchill was hailed as a hero for his refusal to consider surrender, even during the darkest days of the Battle of Britain, when a German invasion seemed imminent.

- Churchill was knighted by Queen Elizabeth II in 1953 and became Sir Winston Churchill.
- Churchill's frequent public appearances during the war helped maintain British morale.
- During the war, Churchill made some of the most famous speeches in British history.
- Churchill was skilled at selecting the best military commanders to lead the Allied war effort.

Timeline

After Adolf Hitler came to power in Germany in 1933, Winston Churchill had warned that he was dangerous. Churchill became Hitler's direct rival when he became prime minister in May 1940.

1933

German Chancellor
Adolf Hitler uses the success of his Nazi Party in the general election to get President Hindenburg to appoint him chancellor. He soon seizes dictatorial powers.

1936

Rearmament
In defiance of the Versailles Treaty, Hitler begins to rearm the German military and to increase the size of the armed services.

1938

Munich Crisis
European leaders allow Hitler to take over the Sudetenland in Czechoslovakia after he says he will not make further demands. He later seizes the rest of the country.

1939

War Begins
Convinced that Britain and France will not react, Hitler invades Poland on September 1. To his surprise, Britain and France both declare war within days.

1940

Fall of France
German troops conquer Belgium, the Netherlands, and France. The British Army, trapped at the port of Dunkirk, is rescued from the beaches by hundreds of "little ships."

1940

Battle of Britain
In July, the German Luftwaffe begins a campaign to establish air supremacy to allow an invasion of Britain. Pilots of the RAF resist until the offensive is called off in late October.

1941

The Blitz
In September, the Luftwaffe begins a series of intensive nighttime bombing raids on British cities, particularly London, to destroy civilian morale. The Blitz ends in May 1941.

1942

El Alamein
In October, Allied troops being pushed eastward in North Africa make a stand at El Alamein in Egypt. In heavy fighting, they win a decisive victory over the German Afrika Korps.

1944

D-Day
On June 6, 1944, the Allies launch the biggest amphibious invasion in history across the English Channel. By nightfall they have a toehold on the beaches of Normandy in France.

1945

Fall of Berlin
In April, Soviet troops fight their way into Berlin. On April 30, Hitler kills himself in his underground bunker. On May 8, Germany formally surrenders to the Allies.

Forced Out
In July, Churchill's Conservative Party loses the general election by a landslide to Clement Attlee's Labour Party. Churchill will return as prime minister from 1951 to 1955.

1946

Iron Curtain
In March, Churchill makes a speech in Fulton, Missouri, in which he says an "iron curtain" now divides Europe. Some observers believe the speech marks the start of the Cold War.

Glossary

air supremacy A position in which one side's aircraft can fly without any threat from the other side.

allies Countries that work together to achieve a particular goal.

appeasement A policy of giving in to an opponent's demands in order to avoid any type of conflict.

annex To seize territory and make it part of one's own territory.

anti-Semitic Based on an irrational hatred of Jews.

buffer zone A neutral area that separates hostile neighbors.

bunker A reinforced underground shelter.

capitalism A political system based on economic and personal freedom.

communism A political system that promotes the limiting of personal property and state control of the economy.

conscription Compulsory service in the armed forces.

dictator A ruler who has complete control over a country.

dogfight A close one-on-one combat between military aircraft of opposing sides.

fascist Following a political system based on a lack of personal freedom and total intolerance of dissent.

flotilla A small fleet of ships or boats.

glider A light aircraft that flies without an engine.

Luftwaffe The German Air Force in World War II.

morale The spirit of a person or a group of people and their confidence about achieving a particular purpose.

negotiate To bargain or come to an agreement with someone.

paramilitary A group that is organized along military lines.

paratroopers Soldiers who parachute from aircraft.

propaganda Information used to support or criticize a particular political point of view.

radar A system that uses radio waves to detect the location of objects.

strategy A plan of action to achieve a long-term goal rather than an immediate result.

Further Resources

Books

Alternator Books. *Heroes of Dunkirk*. Lerner Publishing, 2019.

Bains, Alisha. *World War II. A Political and Diplomatic History of the Modern World.* Rosen Publishing, 2017.

Dickman, Nancy. *The Horror of World War II.* Capstone Publishing, 2018.

Freeburg, Jessica. *Fight for Survival: The Story of the Holocaust.* Capstone Publishing, 2017.

New York Times Editorial Staff. *Adolf Hitler. Public Profiles.* Rosen Publishing, 2019.

Smith, David. *100 Inspirational Quotes by Winston Churchill.* Independently published, 2021.

Websites

www.historyplace.com/worldwar2/defeat/index.html
The History Place index of pages telling the full story of the defeat of Adolf Hitler.

www.spiegel.de/international/europe/the-man-who-saved-europe-how-winston-churchill-stopped-the-nazis-a-712259.html
A detailed account of Winston Churchill's role in the defeat of Hitler from the respected German magazine *Der Spiegel*.

www.bbc.co.uk/history/battle_of_britain/
A BBC site with links and videos telling the story of the Battle of Britain, including Churchill's refusal to surrender.

www.historyextra.com/feature/churchills-greatest-speeches
The BBC History Magazine presents extracts from Churchill's greatest wartime speeches and explains the context in which he made them.

Publisher's note to educators and parents: Our editors have carefully reviewed these websites to ensure that they are suitable for students. Many websites change frequently, however, and we cannot guarantee that a site's future contents will continue to meet our high standards of quality and educational value. Be advised that students should be closely supervised whenever they access the Internet.

Index